Max Fox at The Hut

By Carmel Reilly

Max Fox has a sax.

The sax has a big box.

Max lugs the box
to The Hut.

The gig is here at six.

Max met Rox and Zac
at The Hut.

Max, Rox and Zac set up for the gig.

Max lets the sax rip!

The fans hop and bop.

The fans hop and bop a lot!

Max had lots of fun.

But Max can not lug
his sax box.

CHECKING FOR MEANING

1. What did Max Fox have in the big box? *(Literal)*

2. Who did Max meet at The Hut? *(Literal)*

3. Why couldn't Max lug his sax box home? *(Inferential)*

EXTENDING VOCABULARY

lug	What does *lug* mean? What is another word you know that has the same or similar meaning?
sax	What is a *sax*? What is the full name of this musical instrument? Why do we sometimes use this short form of the word?
Yip	What sounds are in this word? What does it mean? What other words can you use when you call out excitedly?

MOVING BEYOND THE TEXT

1. How do you play a sax? What are other instruments you can play by blowing them?

2. What do people do when they go to a gig?

3. Who do you think is the leader of the band? Why?

4. Why are lots of musical instruments kept in a case or a box?

SPEED SOUNDS

Xx	Yy	Zz				
Kk	Ll	Vv	Qq	Ww		
Dd	Jj	Oo	Gg	Uu		
Cc	Bb	Rr	Ee	Ff	Hh	Nn
Mm	Ss	Aa	Pp	Ii	Tt	

PRACTICE WORDS

Fox

Max

sax

box

Yip

yip

six

Yes

Zac

Rox